DATE DUE

AUG 1 0 1994		
AUG 1 0 1994		

The Library Store   #47-0103

JUST LOOK AT....

THE UNIVERSE

JUST LOOK AT...
THE UNIVERSE

Neil Ardley

Rourke Enterprises, Inc.
Vero Beach, FL 32964
Distributed by Marshall Cavendish

Factual Adviser: Mrs Susan Becklake

Editors: Suzanne Greene and Polly Dunnett
Teacher Panel: John Allen, Diane Jackson, Lynne McCoombe
Designer: Ewing Paddock
Production: Rosemary Bishop
Picture Research: Diana Morris

Illustrations
Roy Bentley 14, 20, 27, 39
Peter Dennis (Linda Rogers Associates) 8–9, 10,
11, 12, 13, 24–25
Jeremy Gower (B.L. Kearley Ltd) 28–29, 30–31,
32–33, 34–35, 40–41
Kuo Kang Chen 14–15, 18–19, 21, 36, 38–39
Mark Lewis 16–17

Photographs
Associated Press: 35.
BPCC: NASA 19l; Cal. Tech. & Carnegie Inst.,
Washington 21r, 29, 37t.
Bob Estall: 43.
Michael Holford: 8–9, 11.
Lick Observatory: 39t.
Courtesy MMT Observatory, Arizona: 13.
NASA: 22–23, 23r.
Palomar Observatory: 33.
Picturepoint: 24.
Photo Library International: 31.
Popperfoto: 42.
Science Photo Library: cover, title page,
contents page, 15, 19r, 20–21, 23b, 26, 37b,
39 inset.

Title page photo: The Horsehead Nebula
Contents page photo: The Kitt Peak Observatory,
Arizona

Library of Congress Cataloging in Publication Data

Ardley, Neil.
  The universe.

  (Just look at . . .)
  Summary: A history of astronomy, technology in
astronomy, stars, the solar system, and the advent of
man in space.
  1. Astronomy—Juvenile literature. [1. Universe.
2. Astronomy. 3. Space flight] I. Title. II. Series.
QB46.A68 1985   520   85-19336
ISBN 0-86592-951-3

How to use this book
Look first in the contents page to see if the subject you want is listed. For instance, if you want to find out about the Sun and the Moon you will find the information on pages 18 and 19. The word list explains the more difficult terms found in this book. The index will tell you how many times a particular subject is mentioned and whether there is a picture of it.

The Universe is one of a series of books on Science and Technology. All the books on this subject have a red color band around the cover. If you want to know more about space and technology, look for other books with a red band in the **Just Look At. . .** series.

CONTENTS

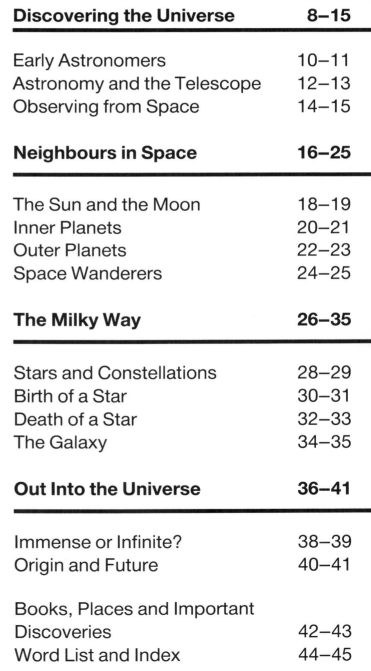

DISCOVERING THE UNIVERSE

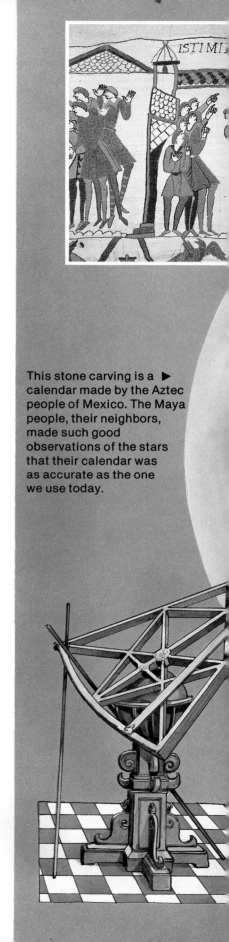

The universe is everything that exists. Our world, the Earth, is only a tiny part of the whole universe, which incudes the Moon, all the planets out in space, the Sun, the stars that shine in the night sky, and also mysterious objects like "black holes." To look out into the universe, all you have to do is peer up into the sky on a clear night. Of course, people have been doing this since prehistoric times. Astronomy, the study of the universe, is probably the oldest science of all.

Ancient peoples looked at the heavens in fear and wonder for they believed them to be the home of gods who ruled their lives. Even today many people read their horoscopes, which are based on the idea that the stars somehow influence the way we are and what happens to us.

For a long time people have also had practical reasons for gazing into the sky. They found out how long a day and a year last by observing how the Sun and stars move in the sky. In this way, people were first able to measure time so that clocks and calendars could be made.

Astronomers have learned much about the universe by using telescopes. Now, spacecraft are taking instruments and people away from the Earth and out into the universe. The knowledge gained over many centuries will not seem so great compared with the new discoveries that space flight will bring.

This stone carving is a ▶ calendar made by the Aztec people of Mexico. The Maya people, their neighbors, made such good observations of the stars that their calendar was as accurate as the one we use today.

In ancient Egypt, people believed that the sky goddess Nut stretched her starry body across the heavens. The Sun, god, Ra, sailed over her in a boat from east to west every day while the Earth god, Geb, lay below. ▶

◄ Because they disturbed the heavens, comets were once thought to bring disaster. The appearance of Halley's comet in 1066 is shown in the Bayeux tapestry and King Harold is shown being told about it. Shortly after, the Normans invaded Britain and King Harold died in battle.

◄ The launch of the Space Shuttle began a new era in spaceflight. Today more people are flying in space and studying the universe from space than ever before.

Stonehenge is an ancient monument in southern England. It was built about 4,000 years ago. Some of its stones line up with the positions of the Sun and the Moon at certain times of the year, and Stonehenge may have been used to observe them in order to find the date, rather as we use a calendar. ▼

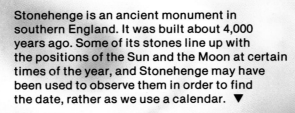

◄ Sextants were used by early astronomers to measure the positions of the Sun, Moon, planets and stars in the sky.

Early Astronomers

Today, astronomers use telescopes and other scientific instruments to study the stars. However, much knowledge of the universe was gained long before the invention of the telescope. The early astronomers used simple instruments like quadrants to observe and measure the positions of the stars in the sky. They also noted the time at which certain stars lined up with particluar objects such as mountains and standing stones.

Ancient observatories

The bigger the instruments, the more accurrate they were. Observations were built at places all around the world to house huge instruments. By the time the telescope was invented, nearly 400 years ago, the positions of the stars in the sky were known with great accuracy.

The stars always appear to keep the same distance from each other in the sky, so they were called the "fixed stars". The early astronomers also noted that the Sun, Moon and planets all seem to move slowly through the background of fixed stars and they could see, too, that the whole sky seems to rotate in a full circle once every day.

Reasons and results

The early astronomers could not find out any more than this about the universe by observation. They could not visit the Moon, for example, or use telescopes and space probes to get a close look at the planets. Neither could they make accurate measurements of, say, the distances of the Sun or the stars from the Earth. They looked at the results of their observations and used them to work out theories about what the universe was really like.

Much of this work took place in ancient Greece, over 2000 years ago. The astronomers realized that the stars must be far away, though they had no idea just how distant they are. They knew that the background of fixed stars appears to rotate because the Earth itself spins. Eratosthenes, a Greek astronomer, showed that the Earth is round and worked out its correct size in 240 B.C.

The way in which the Moon appears to change shape from night to night, growing from a thin crescent to a round disc, and then shrinking again, showed that the Moon must orbit, or revolve around, the Earth. The apparent movements of the Sun and planets against the stars were not so easy to explain.

◀ Early astronomers used quadrants to observe the heavens. They looked along the arm of the instrument and lined it up with a star.

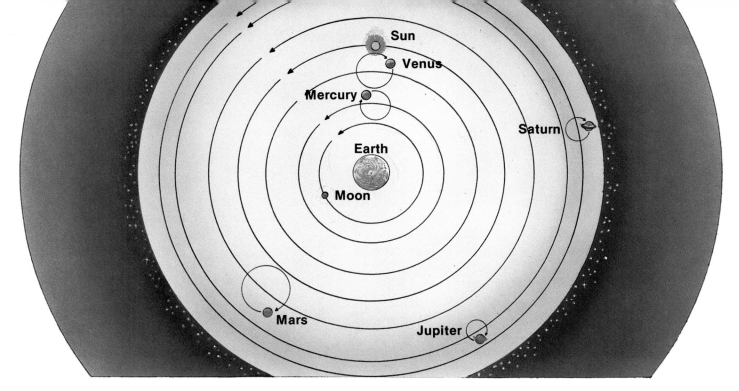

▲ In about A.D. 150, the Greek astronomer Ptolemy wrote that the Sun, Moon and planets move in circles around the Earth. To explain why the planets seem to move against the stars, Ptolemy said that they must revolve in small circles at the same time.

The center of the universe

Because stars could be seen in all directions, the early astronomers thought that the Earth must be at the center of the universe. It seemed that the movements of the Sun and planets against the stars must happen because they revolved around the Earth, like the Moon but farther away.

However, there was a problem. The movements of the planets are strange; sometimes they change direction and move backward against the stars! This could not happen if they moved in circles around the Earth. The early astronomers were puzzled by this problem, and to explain it most of them insisted that the planets moved in circles within circles.

One person, an ancient Greek astronomer called Aristarchus, had the true solution. He said in about 250 B.C. that the Earth and planets all move around the Sun. This easily explained the movements of the planets in the sky, but no one would believe that the Earth was not the center of the universe.

▲ The old observatory at Jaipur, India, contains large stone constructions that were used for measuring the positions of the stars in the sky. With their results, the astronomers could measure time and predict eclipses.

Astronomy and the Telescope

The telescope was invented in Holland in 1608. Within a few months, the great astronomer Galileo used one to observe the sky. The magnified view that he obtained of the Moon and planets gave him the feeling that he had leaped out into space to look at these worlds from near by. The telescope has allowed astronomers to do this ever since. As instruments have improved, so we have been able to explore farther and farther out into the universe.

Galileo's discoveries

The discoveries that Galileo made with his telescopes mark the beginning of modern astronomy. He saw that there are mountains on the Moon and realized that it is a round world similar to the Earth. He saw that the planet Venus has phases, or appears to change shape, like the Moon, and that the planet Jupiter has moons revolving around it.

◀ Galileo started building telescopes as soon as he heard that one had been invented in Holland, and he was the first to use them to study the night sky.

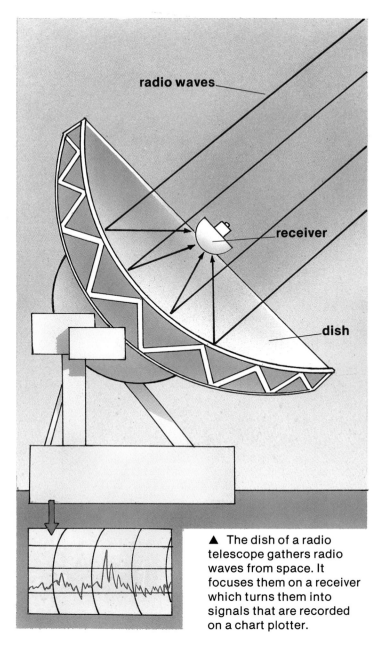

radio waves

receiver

dish

▲ The dish of a radio telescope gathers radio waves from space. It focuses them on a receiver which turns them into signals that are recorded on a chart plotter.

Many large telescopes have huge curved mirrors to capture the faint light from distant stars and galaxies. The new multiple mirror telescope has a set of small, computer controlled mirrors which are as powerful as one large mirror, but cheaper to build. ▼

Galileo's observations of the planets convinced him that the Earth and all the planets must revolve around the Sun. The Polish astronomer, Nicolaus Copernicus, had already published this theory in 1543, but most people still would not accept it. Galileo's support for Copernicus convinced many, but they were not proved right until 1728, when evidence of the Earth's movement was found. Then, at last, our ideas about the universe began to be more accurate.

New discoveries
Astronomers built telescopes with more and more power to see ever farther into the universe. They discovered objects too faint to be seen by the naked eye, that is, without the aid of any instrument. New planets were found: Uranus in 1781, Neptune in 1846 and Pluto in 1930. As well as thousands of stars that had not been seen before, astronomers also discovered things like nebulae, which are growing clouds of gas and dust, far away in space.

The universe "grew" as astronomers discovered bodies (the term used for any object in the universe) farther and farther from the Earth. Late in the 1700s, they realized that the Sun is only one of millions of stars in a huge group of stars called the galaxy. Then, in this century, galaxy upon galaxy has been found, far beyond our own galaxy, in all directions. We now know the universe is truly enormous, perhaps even infinite in size.

Invisible astronomy
The distant stars that we can see with the naked eye or with ordinary telescopes send out rays of light that travel to us across space. However, there are also invisible rays that stream through space from stars, galaxies and other bodies. Among them are radio waves, which astronomers can detect with radio telescopes. The radio "pictures" that they get can show new objects invisible to telescopes.

Observing from Space

If you look through a telescope at a distant planet you may feel as though you are far away in space, observing the planet from near by. Of course you are really stuck firmly to the surface of the Earth and the Earth's atmosphere is always above you. Any light from space must pass through the atmosphere before it reaches you, and as it does so the atmosphere distorts the light rays.

This distortion makes the stars twinkle and it blurs the pictures that telescopes produce. This is why observatories are built at the tops of high mountains. Not only is the sky normally clear of clouds, but there is also less air above for light rays from the stars to pass through.

However, now that we can travel into space we can get a much clearer view of the universe than ever before because, in space, there is no air to distort light rays. Furthermore, in space there are

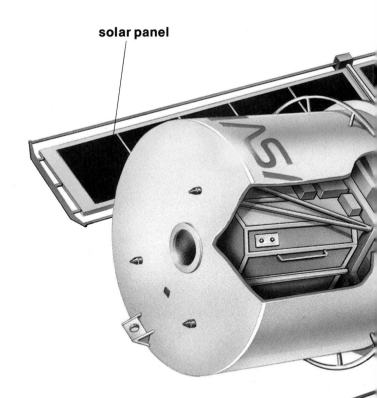

solar panel

The Space Telescope is controlled ▶ by radio from the ground. The telescope is pointed in a particular direction. Its lid opens and then the curved mirror forms an image that is sent as radio signals from the dish shaped antennae to the ground. The telescope gets its power from the large solar panels. It is 39 feet long and weighs about 22,000 pounds.

The Earth's atmosphere bends the light rays that come from distant stars. This means that from the surface of the Earth you can never get a completely clear picture of a distant star.

other rays produced by the Sun, planets, stars and galaxies that do not get through the Earth's atmosphere at all. In space, we can pick up these invisible rays and new kinds of observations can be made. Pictures from space can be taken by astronauts in spacecraft. In addition there are satellites, which are automatic spacecraft that orbit the Earth, and contain instruments that can send pictures back to the ground.

Astronomical satellites

The instruments on a satellite point at a body and capture the invisible rays, such as X-rays, ultraviolet and infra-red rays, coming from it. They form a picture which is sent to the ground by radio. The computer turns the radio signals into a TV picture or photograph. It can add colors to show up the different strengths of the invisible rays.

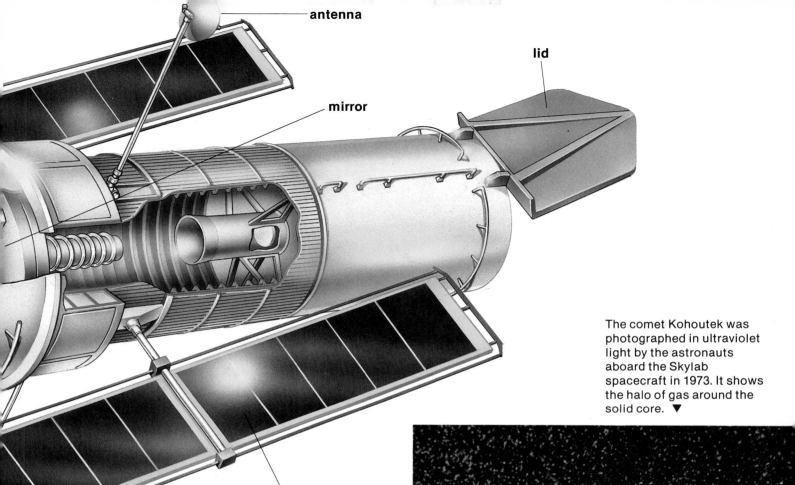

antenna

lid

mirror

solar panel

The comet Kohoutek was photographed in ultraviolet light by the astronauts aboard the Skylab spacecraft in 1973. It shows the halo of gas around the solid core. ▼

From these pictures, astronomers can make many discoveries. They can look into the interior of the Sun by taking an X-ray picture. Ultraviolet pictures make it possible to measure the amount of dust floating in space. Infra-red pictures of some nearby stars show that they are surrounded by dust and rocks from which planets may be forming.

The Space Telescope
In 1986, a new kind of telescope will begin to observe the universe. It is the Space Telescope, a large telescope that will be taken into orbit by the Space Shuttle. It could be as important in our discovery of the universe as Galileo's telescopes were. Because it will work in space, this telescope will detect objects 50 times fainter than the faintest that can be seen from the ground. Through it, we may be able to see seven times farther away than we can now.

NEIGHBORS IN SPACE

Our world, the Earth, is one of the nine major planets that orbit, or revolve around, the Sun. Like the Earth, most of these planets have at least one moon revolving around them. Also moving around the Sun are very small bodies called asteroids, or minor planets, and balls of gas and dust called comets. All these bodies "belong" to the Sun. The light of the Sun shines on them and its heat warms them. The Sun also holds them in their orbits by its powerful gravity, which is the natural force that causes one body to be pulled toward another.

Together with the Sun, all these objects make up the Solar System. Our nearest neighbor is always the Moon, which is much nearer than any other world. Of the planets, Venus comes nearer to us than any other. When it is near, it looks like a very bright star, low in the sky.

People knew about the five nearest planets in ancient times. This was because they could see them with the naked eye. The three outer planets are much fainter. For centuries, people though that the Moon and planets might be like the Earth and that beings of some kind might live on them. When space probes began to visit them from the early 1960s onward, it soon became clear that none of the other planets are like the Earth. Elsewhere in the Solar System, it is either far too hot or too cold for life as we know it to exist.

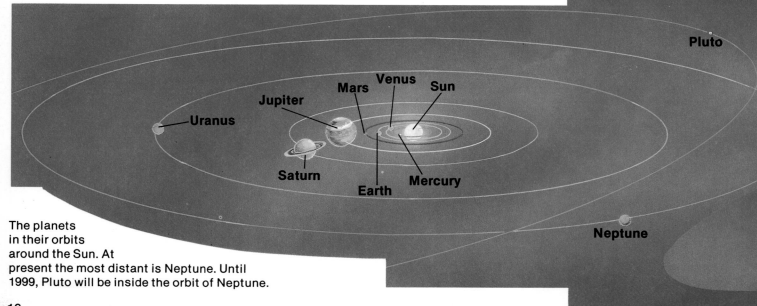

The planets in their orbits around the Sun. At present the most distant is Neptune. Until 1999, Pluto will be inside the orbit of Neptune.

The planets of the Solar System. The largest is Jupiter, which has 11 times the diameter of Earth. Pluto is the smallest planet, and it may be only a quarter the size of the Earth. All the planets are small compared with the Sun, which is 109 times bigger in diameter than the Earth.

Sun

Saturn

Mercury

Venus

Earth

Mars

Jupiter

The Sun and the Moon

To us, the Sun and the Moon are the most important bodies in the heavens. Apart from comets that approach the Earth, all the other objects in the universe appear to the naked eye only as tiny points of light.

The nearest star

The Sun is in fact a star. It is the nearest star of all and compared with the other stars it is average in size. We see it as a round disc rather than a tiny point of light because it is much nearer to us than any other star.

The Sun shines so brightly that its light prevents us from seeing any other stars or the planets during the day. All life on the Earth exists only because the Sun provides just the right amount of light and heat. You should never look directly at the Sun as its light could damage your eyes.

A dead world

The Moon gives us some light too, but moonlight does not really come from the Moon. The Moon shines because it is lit by the Sun, and moonlight is in fact reflected sunlight.

The Moon appears to change shape slowly as it moves around the Earth. It goes from a crescent to a disc and back again, and sometimes does not shine at all. This happens because, as it moves, the sunlit side of the Moon comes into view and then slowly disappears. These changes are called the phases of the Moon.

The Moon is a dead world. It has no air or water and so no life at all. Its surface gets as hot as boiling water when the Sun shines on it, but far colder than freezing when it is dark there. The astronauts who landed on the Moon from 1969 to 1972 had to wear spacesuits to survive.

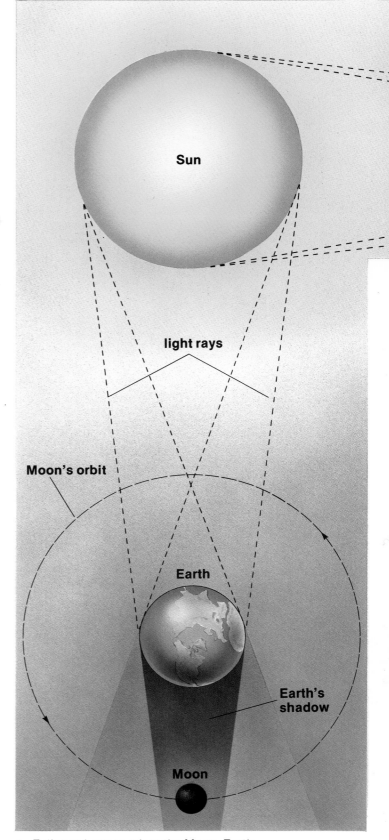

▲ Eclipses happen when the Moon, Earth and Sun are exactly in line. When an eclipse of the Moon takes place, the Moon passes through the Earth's shadow.

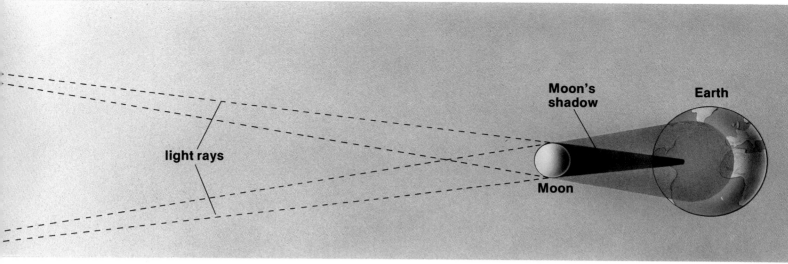

light rays

Moon's shadow

Earth

Moon

The American astronauts landed on the Moon to carry out scientific experiments there. They collected and brought back many rocks to help scientists find out how the Moon formed. ▼

▲ When an eclipse of the Sun happens, the Moon's shadow touches the Earth's surface. In the area of shadow, the Sun is blotted out by the Moon. Elsewhere, part of the Sun's disc may be blotted out in a partial eclipse.

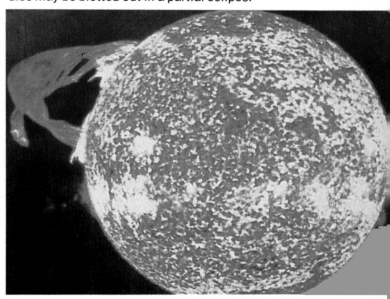

▲ The surface of the Sun is turbulent, or stormy. This picture shows a great burst of flame called a solar prominence shooting out from the Sun.

Eclipses and tides

The Moon is much smaller than the Sun but much nearer to us. It appears to be exactly the same size as the Sun. Because of this, an amazing thing sometimes happens: a total eclipse of the Sun. In this kind of eclipse, the Moon passes exactly in front of the Sun. It blots out the Sun's disc but the bright gas surrounding the Sun suddenly becomes visible. Unfortunately, a total eclipse of the Sun is very rare.

The Moon can be eclipsed too. This happens when it passes into the Earth's shadow and disappears from view for a short time. Eclipses of the Moon are much more frequent than eclipses of the Sun, and happen about twice a year.

The Sun and Moon also affect the Earth in another way. Their forces of gravity pull slightly on the Earth and raise the water in the sea, causing the tides. The tides rise and fall every day because the Earth rotates.

Inner Planets

A total of nine planets, including the Earth, move around the Sun. The planets are large, round worlds, like the Earth. Most of the other planets have an atmosphere, but none of them have air or water as on the Earth. We can see the planets in the night sky. To the naked eye they look like stars. They are not stars and they do not produce any light of their own. Like the Moon, they are lit by the Sun.

Most of our knowledge of the planets has been gained by space probes. These automatic spacecraft have flown past, orbited around or landed on five of the planets, and they have sent back pictures and information to us by radio.

The four planets nearest to the Sun are known as the inner planets. They are all small worlds compared with the other planets, and the Earth is the largest of them. The other inner planets are Mercury, Venus and Mars.

The Moonlike planet
Mercury is the planet nearest to the Sun and it is very like our Moon. It has almost no atmosphere and life cannot exist there. Mercury has a rocky surface that is covered with craters. These craters

▲ Sunset on Mars, as viewed by the Viking 1 space probe.

could have been caused by pieces of rock called meteroids crashing into Mercury from space. Or they may be the result of volcanic eruptions.

The evening star
Venus is known as the "evening star" because it is often the first "star" to be seen in the sky as it gets dark. It is not a star, but a planet almost the same size as the Earth. However, everything else about Venus is different from the Earth.

Venus is permanently covered in thick white cloud. The atmosphere contains gases that we could not breathe, and it collects the Sun's heat, making the surface of Venus the hottest place in the Solar System apart from the Sun itself.

You couldn't send a postcard home from Venus. It's so hot there that a plastic pen would melt within seconds!

▲ The surface of Mercury as seen by
Mariner 10. This space probe only took
pictures of half of Mercury. However, the rest
is very likely to look much the same.

Russian space probes landed on Venus in 1975
and sent back pictures of a rocky terrain. Space
probes in orbit around Venus have made maps of
the planet. It has a huge plain and two large
highland regions that probably contain active
volcanoes. There are no oceans.

The red planet

The fourth planet, Mars, is about half the size of
the Earth. It is called the red planet because it
looks reddish and when two space probes landed
there in 1976, they found that the rocks on the
surface of Mars are in fact red. The atmosphere is
thin and unbreathable and it is mostly cold.

Mars is interesting because probably there was
once liquid water on its surface. However, all the
water is now frozen in the polar ice caps. There
are deep canyons on Mars, in which there may
once have been rivers, but the planet is now a dry,
rocky, lifeless desert, dotted with huge mountains
and craters.

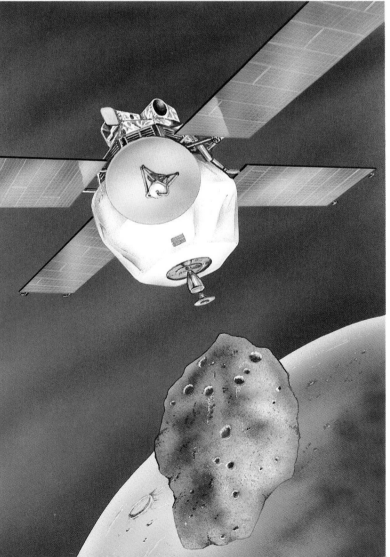

◄ Phobos, one of the two moons of Mars,
is examined by the space probe, Mariner 9,
in orbit around Mars. Both moons are only a
few miles across.

Outer Planets

The five outer planets of the Sun's family are all far from the Sun, orbiting slowly in the cold, dark, remote regions of the Solar System. And all but one are huge worlds, very different from the inner planets, with atmospheres of unbreathable gases. Many moons orbit around them, all probably as lifeless as our Moon.

The giant planet
The nearest of the outer planets is Jupiter, and it is also the biggest of all the planets. Pioneer and Voyager probes have flown past Jupiter sending us marvellous pictures of the planet and its moons. Jupiter is completely covered with one enormous ocean of liquid hydrogen. The atmosphere above contains belts of cloud that surround the whole planet. A huge, continuous storm called The Great Red Spot is in one of these belts.

Jupiter has at least sixteen moons, four of which are worlds about the size of Mercury or our Moon. Three are covered with ice while the fourth, Io, is bright orange-red in color, and covered in active volcanoes.

The fairest planet
The next planet is Saturn. It is almost as big as Jupiter and has a similar structure, plus a large family of moons. It also has a magnificent set of rings that surround the planet. The rings make Saturn the most beautiful of all the planets.

Saturn's rings are made of countless chunks of ice. They are clustered together and move in orbits around Saturn, forming a wide but very thin series of rings. The origin of the rings is a mystery. Other planets also have rings but so far as we know none are so spectacular as Saturn's. Jupiter's ring is narrow and made of dust.

The depths of the Solar System
The three outermost planets are, in order, Uranus, Neptune and Pluto. Uranus and Neptune are large worlds, several times larger than the Earth. The surfaces of these planets are very cold, and are probably covered with gases in their liquid or frozen form. Both planets have rings and moons.

Pluto is just as cold but otherwise very different. It is the smallest planet, probably smaller than our Moon. It moves in an unusual path around the Sun so that it sometimes comes nearer to us than Neptune. It is possible that Pluto was once a moon of Neptune, but escaped some time in the past. Pluto has one moon called Charon.

Io, the orange-red moon of Jupiter, has active volcanoes all over its surface. The blue cloud in this picture is a volcanic eruption. The photograph was taken by the Voyager 1 space probe. ▶

◄ This close-up view of Saturn reveals the rings in all their glory. The picture was taken by a Voyager space probe as it flew past Saturn and sent back signals to the Earth by radio. You can also see some of Saturn's moons which show up as tiny points of light.

This is the first picture of the rings of Uranus. It was taken with a telescope in 1984 and has been processed by computer. This is why the photograph looks so strange. The rings can be seen immediately around the planet, and some of the moons of Uranus are also shown and labelled. ▼

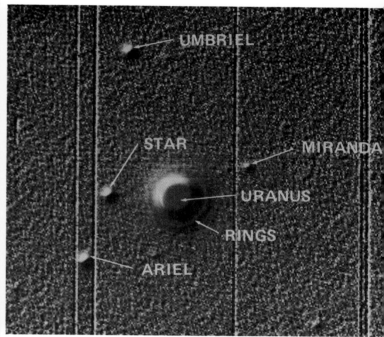

UMBRIEL

STAR

MIRANDA

URANUS

RINGS

ARIEL

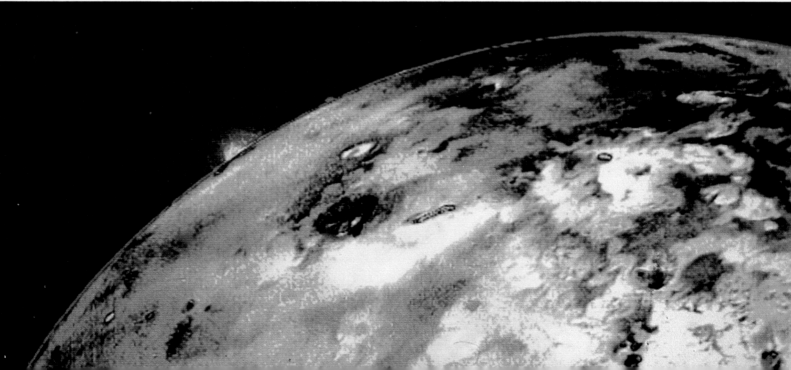

Space Wanderers

The planets and their moons are not the only objects in the Solar System. There are other bodies such as asteroids, comets and meteoroids. Some of these wander through space, and approach or even crash into the Earth and planets.

The asteroids

Asteroids are also known as minor planets. They are not large round worlds like the Earth and other major planets. They are big lumps of rock orbiting the Sun. Many thousands of asteroids are known. The largest asteroid, Ceres, is just over six miles across, but many are only a few thousand feet.

Most of these minor planets have orbits between Mars and Jupiter. Some move in toward the Sun and then out again. The asteroid Icarus, for example, gets so close to the Sun that it must glow red-hot.

▲ Halley's comet takes 76 years to orbit the Sun. It will approach the Sun in 1986, but we will not get a good view of the comet because it will not come very near the Earth. However, space probes such as Giotto will be launched to intercept Halley's comet and send us close-up pictures of it.

◄ Meteor Crater in Arizona, U.S.A., formed when a huge meteorite struck the ground about 22,000 years ago. The crater is just over 3,200 feet across.

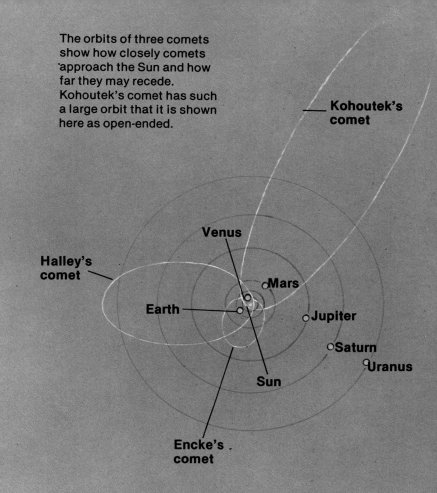

The orbits of three comets show how closely comets approach the Sun and how far they may recede. Kohoutek's comet has such a large orbit that it is shown here as open-ended.

Kohoutek's comet

Venus

Halley's comet

Mars

Earth

Jupiter

Saturn

Uranus

Sun

Encke's comet

Collisions with asteroids are very unlikely but not impossiblie. Asteroids that travel toward and away from the Sun pass across the Earth's orbit and so in theory could hit the Earth itself. In fact, in 1937 the asteroid Hermes did pass fairly close. Some people think that an asteroid may have crashed into the Earth 65 million years ago. If so, it might have caused a change in climate that could explain why the dinosaurs died out.

Comets

Comets are balls of frozen gases and dust. They move in orbits that take them out into the cold, remote regions of the Solar System most of the time, but some comets come in near the Sun every so often. As a comet approaches the Sun, the heat turns some of the gases to vapor and frees some dust. This dust and vapor streams out to form a glowing tail stretching away from the Sun. Then the comet swings around the Sun and begins to travel away. The gases freeze again and the tail then disappears.

Comets may come near the Earth on their way to and from the Sun, and sometimes they can be seen for a short period of time. Some reappear every few years but comets are not a very common sight. Most take centuries to return.

Visitors from space

If you look up into the night sky for long enough, you are likely to see a shooting star. This starlike point of light that races briefly across the sky is not really a star. It is a tiny grain of rock or metal that glows white-hot and burns up as it enters the Earth's atmosphere from space.

These bits of rock and metal are called meteoroids. They orbit the Sun between the planets, and thousands hit the Earth's atmosphere every day, though they only rarely reach the ground. Sometimes one is big enough to survive its flight through the atmosphere and it crashes into the ground. Then it is called a meteorite and, luckily, meteorites are rare.

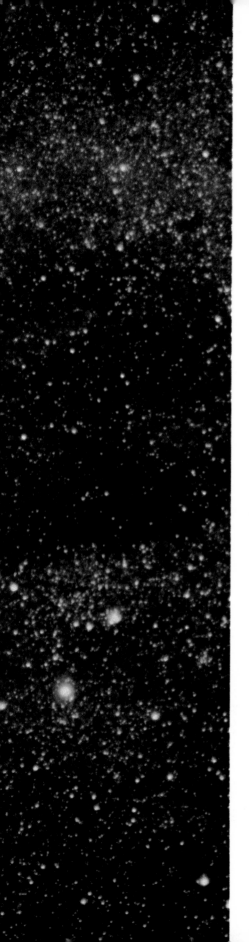

THE MILKY WAY

If you look up into the night sky on a very clear night (you need to be in the country, well away from the bright lights of a city) you will see what looks like a cloudy band stretching across the heavens. This is called the Milky Way and in fact it is not cloud but a band of stars. As you gaze at the Milky Way you are looking into an enormous island of millions of stars floating in space.

Our star, the Sun, is one of the stars in this island, which astronomers call the galaxy. All the stars that you can see in the Milky Way are really suns. That is, like our Sun, they are huge balls of burning gas that pour out light and heat. Many of the stars probably have planets orbiting around them, but so far only one planet has been discovered outside the Solar System.

The galaxy is enormous. It is 100 million times the size of the solar system and it must contain many wonders. It is quite possible that somewhere in the galaxy there are other worlds like the Earth. There may also be intelligent life.

Our space probes have explored much of the solar system and now the most distant probe is beginning a long, long voyage into the galaxy. It is no longer sending back messages, but it carries a picture of a man and a woman as well as scientific information that will tell any other beings who may find it about ourselves.

◄ There are millions of stars in the Milky Way. This small part of it, seen through a telescope, contains a dark nebula, that blocks our view of some of the stars.

Radio and television signals travel out into space from the Earth. If they had highly sensitive equipment, aliens far away in the galaxy might be able to pick up these signals. The radio waves would take a very long time to reach them, though. ►

Stars and Constellations

With the naked eye you can see up to about 2,000 stars from any place on Earth. These are the stars which are either very bright or are near to us in the galaxy. Millions of fainter or more distant stars can only be seen through telescopes.

The most powerful telescopes can show some huge nearby stars as round discs. However, most stars are so small or so far away that they remain as points of light, even when we look at them through telescopes. The nearest star to the Sun is called Proxima Centauri and it is many millions of miles away. Most stars are very much farther away from us than this.

The nature of stars
Nevertheless, we do know what stars are like. Astronomers can learn a lot about stars by observing their light. The color of a star shows us how hot it is. Blue and white stars are very hot while orange and red stars are less hot than the Sun. The Sun, in fact, is an average kind of star in temperature and size. Some stars are thousands of times brighter than the Sun and others are hundreds of times bigger. Others glow with a dim light, or are little bigger than a planet.

Changing stars
Our Sun shines all the time, year in and year out. Its brightness and size do no change; if they did, life could not continue on the Earth. Many other stars are different in this respect. They grow bigger and smaller regularly, and their brightness varies as they change size.

Several stars appear to us to vary in brightness because they are not one star but two stars close together. The two stars revolve around each other, and as one passes in front of the other, their overall brightness changes.

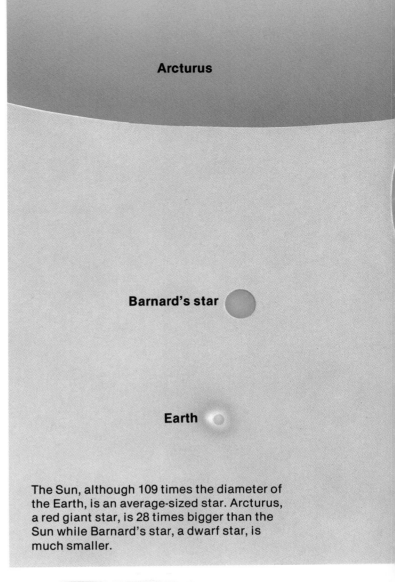

The Sun, although 109 times the diameter of the Earth, is an average-sized star. Arcturus, a red giant star, is 28 times bigger than the Sun while Barnard's star, a dwarf star, is much smaller.

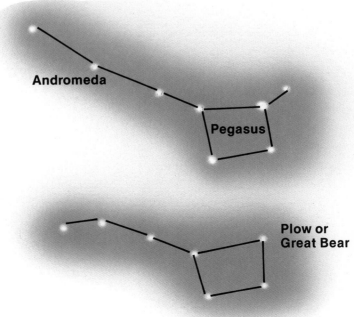

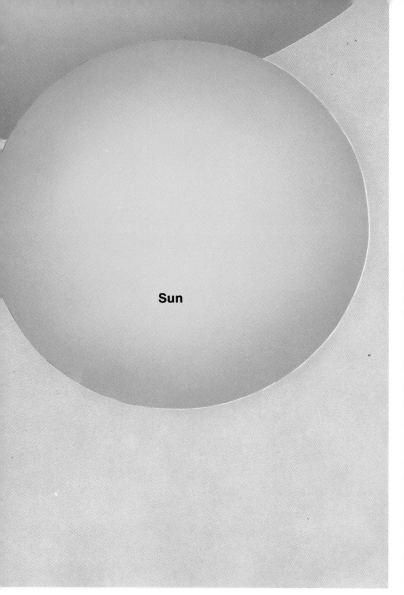

Sun

The Pleiades is a cluster of about 400 stars, at least six of which can be seen with the naked eye. ▼

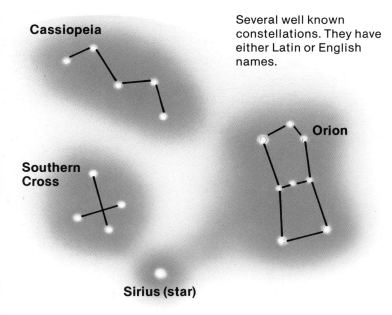

Cassiopeia

Southern
Cross

Orion

Sirius (star)

Several well known constellations. They have either Latin or English names.

Star patterns

The stars form patterns in the sky known as constellations. These were given names long ago and are called after gods, goddesses, heroes, animals and objects. Except for a few constellations such as the Plow, the patterns do not really look like their names. Knowing the constellations does help us to recognize stars as we look up into the night sky.

The constellations are not actual groups of stars in space. They appear to be close together but the stars in a constellation may in fact be very far apart. However, some stars really are comparatively close and form groups called star clusters. The Pleiades is a star cluster that is easy to spot.

Birth of a Star

Stars do not live forever. All around us in the galaxy, stars are being born, living out their lives and dying. Our star, the Sun, is half way through its life. It formed about 5,000 million years ago and it will live about this long again before it dies.

Stars are huge globes of gas so hot that they glow with light. The gas in stars is mostly hydrogen, which is also spread very thinly throughout the space in between stars. Mixed with it are other gases and dust, which may come from stars that died millions of years ago.

Nebulae
The whole galaxy is spinning around and around. As it does so the gas and dust collect in certain places, forming clouds called nebulae. Also, exploding stars send clouds of gases out into space and these may cause nebulae to form.

Inside a cloud, or nebula, the gases and dust particles are pulled slowly together by gravity. Over millions of years, the nebula shrinks and the gases and dust are squeezed together. The nebula breaks up into several smaller clouds that each spin faster and faster as they become still smaller. As the gases in the clouds are squeezed more and more, they get hotter and hotter. Eventually, each separate cloud becomes a globe of glowing gas.

Energy galore
The globe of gas becomes a star when the hydrogen gas at its center reaches a temperature of 10 million degrees Celsius. At this point the high temperature and pressure cause the hydrogen to begin to change into helium, another gas. This change is called nuclear fusion and it produces enormous amounts of energy that the star gives out as heat and light.

A star begins life as a huge cloud of gas and dust floating in space.

The cloud begins to shrink as the force of gravity pulls the grains of dust and particles of gas together.

The Great Nebula is a ► huge cloud of glowing gas in which stars are forming. The nebula can be seen with the naked eye as a misty patch in the constellation of Orion.

The temperature at the star's core rises still further, reaching about 13 million degrees in a star like the Sun but even more in bigger stars. Now the energy produced in the star prevents it from growing any smaller, and it remains the same size, pouring out heat and light into space.

The stars drift apart as they form and sometimes they become single stars, like the Sun. In most cases, pairs of stars remain together like twins and then they are known as double stars. A planet orbiting a double star would have two suns in its sky! Occasionally several stars stay close together to form a cluster of stars.

Solar systems

As a star is born, not all of the cloud always contracts to form the star. A huge ring of gas and dust may be left rotating around the new star. Just as the original nebula broke up, the ring may break up into spinning clumps of gas and dust particles. These then shrink to form balls of rock surrounded by gases. The young star now has a solar system, or family of planets. Like double stars and clusters, the planets may form with moons or rings. The Earth and Moon, and all the other planets and moons of our Solar System, probably formed in this way, about 4,600 million years ago, when the Sun was a new star.

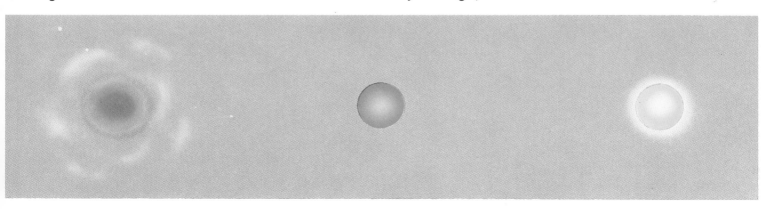

▲ As the cloud shrinks, it begins to heat up.

▲ Eventually, after millions of years, the cloud becomes a ball of hot, glowing gas.

▲ The ball of gas becomes a star when it begins to "burn up" its own gas and radiate heat and light.

Death of a Star

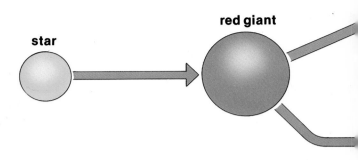

Gradually a star burns up the hydrogen gas of which it is made. When it has used up all its hydrogen fuel, it dies. Bigger stars burn their hydrogen more quickly, so the larger a star is, the shorter its life. Stars die in different ways, depending on their size. The death of a star is always spectacular.

Red giants

Small and average sized stars like the Sun burn steadily for thousands of millions of years. The star then swells into a huge star, maybe a hundred times its former size. The surface cools, causing the star to glow red instead of yellow or white. It is still very hot. When the Sun becomes a red giant star in about 5,000 million years from now, it will burn up the Earth.

The next thing to happen is that the giant star may come apart. The outer layers of gas are pushed out into space and sometimes form a glowing ring. The center of the star, or core, is all that is left behind. It shrinks to only about size of the Earth and shines white-hot. The red giant has turned into a white dwarf star. Over millions of years, the white dwarf cools and its light fades until it becomes a black dwarf, which is a cold, dark globe. It is now invisible against the black background of space.

Exploding stars

A big star may end its days in an even more extraordinary way. After shining for only tens of millions of years, it swells up into a red supergiant. Now the nuclear fusion goes totally out of control. The star destroys itself in a huge explosion, shining brighter than a million Suns for a short time. This explosion is called a supernova and the star has now become an enormous cloud, spreading out through space.

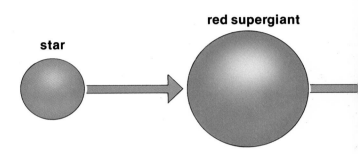

At the same time the core of the star shrinks into a body only the size of a large city. The material in this body is so tightly compressed together that a spoonful of it would weigh many millions of tons. Even more strange, the remains of the star may spin very fast and send out a beam of light or radio waves. This spinning beam seems to flash as we look at it, rather like a lighthouse in space. The spinning star is called a pulsar.

Black holes

A very big star may have the strangest death of all. The star may explode but the core that remains is so big that it collapses in on itself and shrinks to a body only a few thousand feet across. Because it is so small but also very heavy, this body has an enormous force of gravity. Anything that approaches the body is pulled toward it, and can never escape. The gravity is so strong that it even prevents light rays from escaping into space. The body is therefore totally black and because anything falling into it disappears for ever, it is called a black hole.

planetary nebula

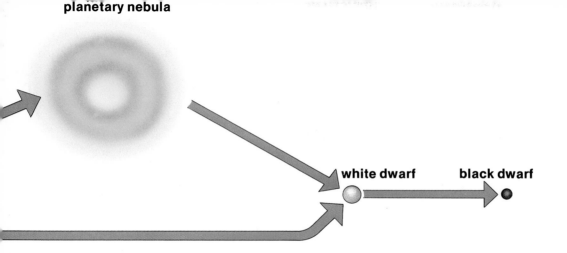

white dwarf   **black dwarf**

◄ When a star is about the same size as the Sun reaches the end of its life, it swells into a red giant star and may then shed its outer layers to produce a glowing ring, or planetary nebula. The remains of the star collapse to form a white dwarf and then a black dwarf star.

supernova

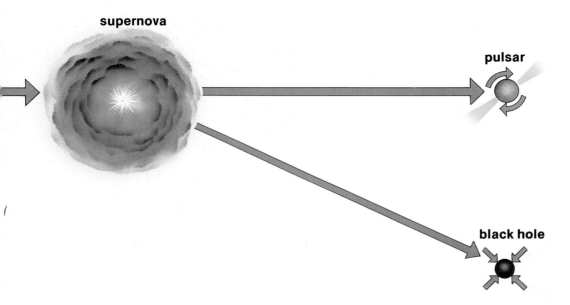

pulsar

black hole

◄ A large star also swells to become a red supergiant at the end of its life. It may then become unstable and explode. At the same time, the remains of the star may collapse to form a pulsar or a black hole.

The Crab Nebula is a cloud of gas and dust formed by the explosion of a star in 1054. At the heart of the nebula, a pulsar has been found flashing on and off 30 times a second. The pulsar is the remains of the original star. ►

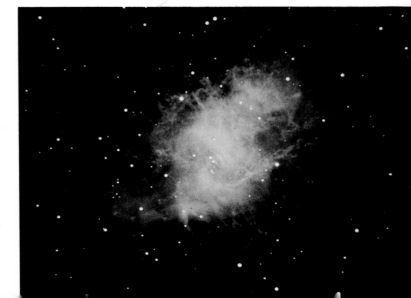

The Galaxy

Once we look outside our solar system it becomes very difficult to measure distances in the normal way. Miles are too small, so instead astronomers use light years. One light year is simply the distance that light travels in a year which is 5.878 trillion miles.

Distances in the galaxy are so large that it is often hard to imagine them. It helps to think of how long light takes to reach the Earth from different places in the galaxy. For example, from the Moon, light takes just over a second to reach us. To get to us from the planets at the edge of the solar system, light travels for about five hours. Light takes more than four years to get from the nearest star to the Sun. And the whole galaxy itself is about 100,000 light years across!

Inside the galaxy

The galaxy contains about 100,000 million stars. It is shaped rather like a huge wheel, but instead of spokes it has "arms" or stars that spiral around a central "hub" of more densely packed stars. The Sun is in one of the spiral arms of stars. It is about 30,000 light years from the center of the galaxy. The whole galaxy is spinning around and around, and the Sun takes 250 million years to travel once around the galaxy. This may seem slow, but the galaxy is so huge that you are in fact moving around it at a speed of about 5,000,000 miles an hour!

We cannot see the center of the galaxy, even with the help of powerful telescopes. This is because of the tiny amounts of gas and dust that float around in the huge empty spaces between the stars. There may be only one molecule, or very small particle, of gas or dust for every inch of space. It is enough to block our view of the center of the galaxy.

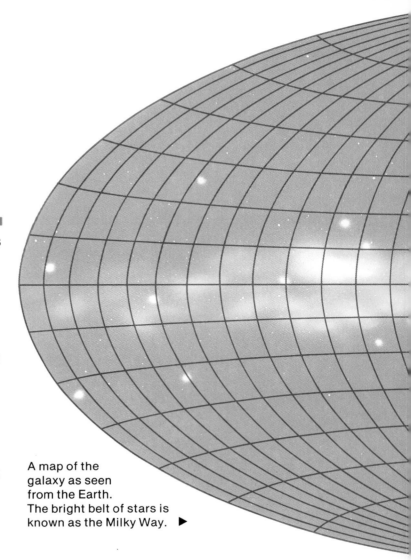

A map of the galaxy as seen from the Earth. The bright belt of stars is known as the Milky Way. ▶

In places, the gas and dust collects together into clouds called nebulae. Some nebulae are bright, either because they glow with light of their own, or because they are lit by stars within them. It is in these bright nebulae that new stars may be forming. Other nebulae are dark.

Exploring the Galaxy

New telescopes and satellites are telling us more and more about the galaxy. In 1983, a satellite called IRAS discovered that several nearby stars have clouds of solid particles around them in which planets may be forming.

The first planet to be discovered outside the solar system was found in 1984. It is in orbit around a nearby star. It is a huge world, about the size of Jupiter, but far hotter than Venus and there is probably no life on it. The space telescope is expected to discover many more planets.

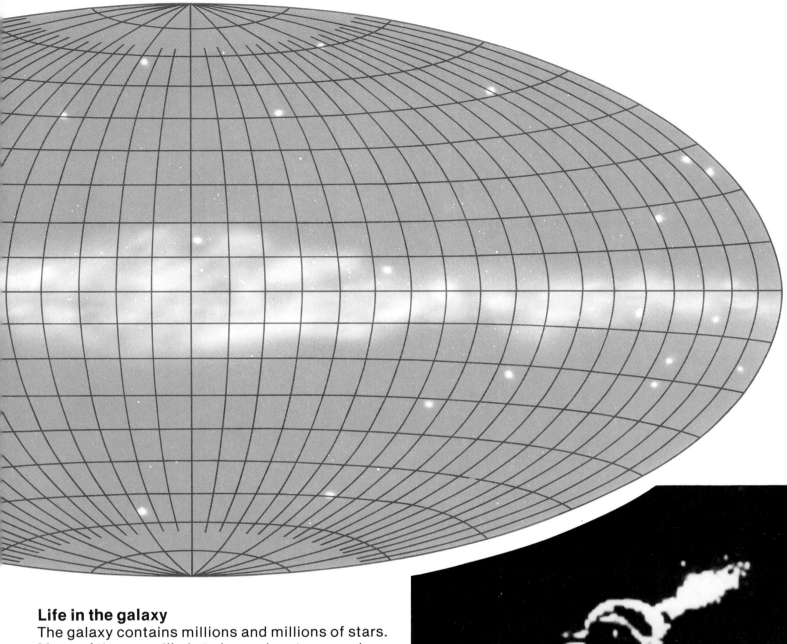

Life in the galaxy

The galaxy contains millions and millions of stars. Many of them are likely to have planets around them. Is it possible that, among all these worlds, some will be like the Earth and have life on them? The answer is yes, but we have no evidence of intelligent life. You might expect distant civilizations to send out radio signals. No signals have yet been picked up from the galaxy.

Even if intelligent beings do exist elsewhere in the galaxy, it would be very difficult to communicate with them. Radio waves travel at the speed of light, so radio signals would take many years to cross the huge distances between any other beings and ourselves. Any spacecraft would travel far slower than light. A journey to the stars would take much longer than a single lifetime.

▲ This photograph, taken by telescope in 1984 and processed by computer, shows a solar system forming around the star Beta Pictoris, which is 50 light years away. It consists of a swarm of particles among which planets may be forming.

OUT INTO THE UNIVERSE

Until the beginning of this century, the galaxy was thought to be the universe. Few people thought that anything could exist beyond the galaxy. The first really powerful telescopes showed amazing things. A nebula in the constellation Andromeda was found to be not a cloud of gas in the galaxy but another whole galaxy of stars. It is bigger than our galaxy, and very distant, over two million light years away. Telescopes and other instruments then revealed more and more galaxies at greater and greater distances from our own. Now millions are known and they have been found in all directions around us. The farthest known objects are thousands of millions of light years away.

Another astonishing discovery was made soon after the first galaxies beyond our own were found. The other galaxies are moving away from us and also from each other. Also, the farther away they are, the faster they appear to be moving. The whole universe is growing larger in every direction!

Will the universe go on getting bigger and bigger for ever and ever? Or will it stop growing at some time in the future? How did the universe form and when did the galaxies begin to move? There are no definite answers to these questions. Astronomers are producing some amazing theories.

elliptical galaxy **spiral galaxy** **barred spiral galaxy**

▲ There are three main kinds of galaxies. Elliptical galaxies are round balls of stars and spiral galaxies (normal and barred) have curved arms of stars. There are also irregular galaxies that have no set shape.

▲ The Andromeda Galaxy is the largest in the group of galaxies around our own galaxy. It is also a spiral galaxy, like our own. The Andromeda galaxy gets its name because it can be seen with the naked eye as a faint patch of light in the constellation of Andromeda.

This picture of a spiral galaxy, has been processed by computer. The computer makes different parts of the galaxy appear in different colors. This produces a more detailed picture than an ordinary photograph. ▶

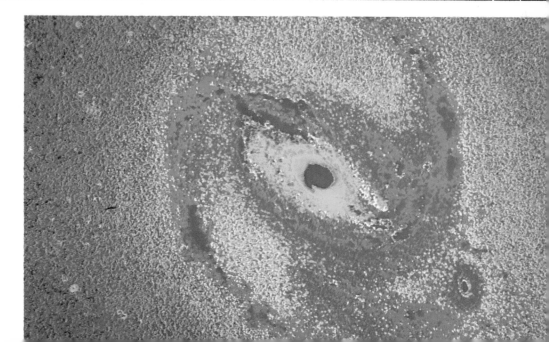

Immense or Infinite?

We have found galaxies at very great distances in all directions around us. Is the universe infinite, so that the galaxies go on for ever? Or does it have a boundary, beyond which nothing exists?

Measuring with light

Even though other galaxies are so far away, astronomers can measure their distances from us. They do this by observing the light that comes from the galaxies. They look at the brightness of certain stars in nearby galaxies. The brighter these stars appear, the nearer the galaxy is to us.

When a galaxy is more distant, astronomers look at the color of the light from the galaxy. The farther away a galaxy is from us, the redder its light appears to be. This redness is caused by the movement of the galaxy away from us. The more distant it is, the faster it moves and the redder its light. This color change is called the red shift.

The most distant objects that we know about are called quasars. Quasars are kinds of galaxies and their red shifts show that they could be thousands of millions of light years away.

Quasars are pouring out huge amounts of light and radio waves. They are as bright as a hundred galaxies put together. Yet all this energy comes from a region in the quasar that is only about the size of our solar system. Some astronomers think that there are black holes in quasars.

The red shifts of faraway quasars show that they could be moving away at very nearly the speed of light. Any objects farther away than this would be moving even faster. Scientists believe that no object can move faster than the speed of light. So it is possible that very few bodies exist beyond the distant quasars, and that these quasars are near the edge of the universe.

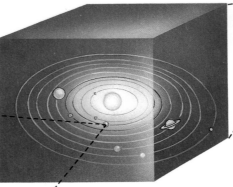

▲ The distance of the nearest stars is 10,000 times the distance across the solar system.

▲ The distance across the solar system is 1,000,000 times the diameter of the Earth.

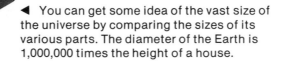

◄ You can get some idea of the vast size of the universe by comparing the sizes of its various parts. The diameter of the Earth is 1,000,000 times the height of a house.

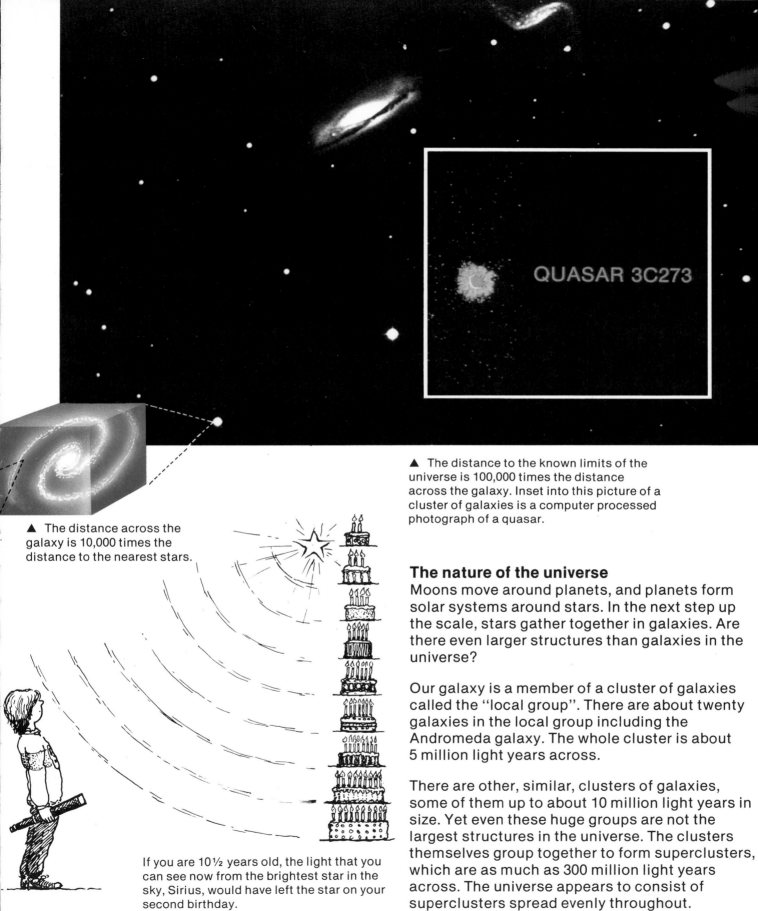

QUASAR 3C273

▲ The distance across the galaxy is 10,000 times the distance to the nearest stars.

▲ The distance to the known limits of the universe is 100,000 times the distance across the galaxy. Inset into this picture of a cluster of galaxies is a computer processed photograph of a quasar.

If you are 10½ years old, the light that you can see now from the brightest star in the sky, Sirius, would have left the star on your second birthday.

The nature of the universe

Moons move around planets, and planets form solar systems around stars. In the next step up the scale, stars gather together in galaxies. Are there even larger structures than galaxies in the universe?

Our galaxy is a member of a cluster of galaxies called the "local group". There are about twenty galaxies in the local group including the Andromeda galaxy. The whole cluster is about 5 million light years across.

There are other, similar, clusters of galaxies, some of them up to about 10 million light years in size. Yet even these huge groups are not the largest structures in the universe. The clusters themselves group together to form superclusters, which are as much as 300 million light years across. The universe appears to consist of superclusters spread evenly throughout.

Origin and Future

We know that the Earth formed about 4,600 million years ago from a cloud of gas and dust. When did the universe form? And how did it begin?

When we look out into the universe, we find millions of galaxies all rushing away from each other. If we think of this movement going backward into the past, then at some time long ago, the galaxies were all close together. Something must have happened to make them begin to move apart and most astronomers believe that what happened not only started the galaxies moving but also formed them. This event, the greatest ever to occur, was the creation of the universe.

The Big Bang
If the galaxies have always been moving apart at the same speed, then they would have been close together about 15,000 million years ago. It is possible that all the material in the universe was then packed into a tiny point. What probably happened next was an enormous explosion, which is known as the Big Bang. It formed hydrogen and helium gases that spread out from the explosion. As the gases moved, they began to form clouds in which galaxies of stars formed. This process of expansion and formation is probably still going on.

The gases still left drifting in space were very, very hot at first. They would have cooled gradually since the Big Bang, but they should still have a little heat left now. This heat would be enough to make them produce weak radio waves throughout space. These radio waves were detected in 1965 by radio telescopes. Their discovery convinced most astronomers that the Big Bang really did happen.

Open, closed or steady?
The universe may be "open"; that is, it will go on expanding and eventually it will die. Or it may be "closed"; that is, the movement will stop and then go into reverse. Possibly a brand new universe would then form, after another Big Bang. Another theory, less popular with astronomers, is that our present universe has always existed and will never end. This is the steady state theory.

If the universe did form in the Big Bang, what existed before? A possible answer is that nothing existed. The Big Bang may have created not only the material of the universe, but also the space and time in which it exists.

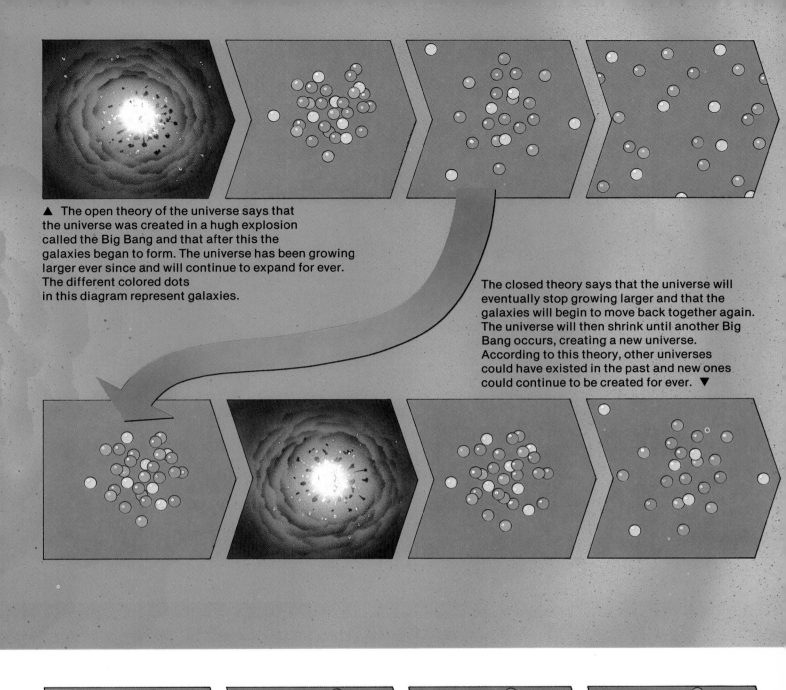

▲ The open theory of the universe says that the universe was created in a hugh explosion called the Big Bang and that after this the galaxies began to form. The universe has been growing larger ever since and will continue to expand for ever. The different colored dots in this diagram represent galaxies.

The closed theory says that the universe will eventually stop growing larger and that the galaxies will begin to move back together again. The universe will then shrink until another Big Bang occurs, creating a new universe. According to this theory, other universes could have existed in the past and new ones could continue to be created for ever. ▼

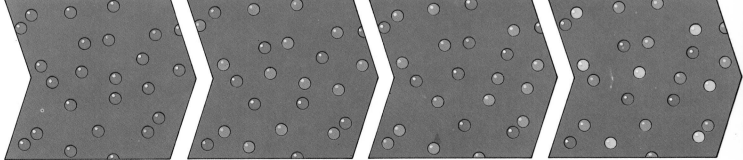

▲ The steady state theory of the universe says that galaxies are always being created and that the universe always grows larger. New galaxies form as old ones move apart.

Books and Places

Books to read
Space Travel (Bendick, Jeanne) F. Watts, 1982
Space Shots, Shuttles, and Satellites (Berger, Melvin) Putnam, 1984
Star Gazing, Comet Tracking, And Sky Mapping (Berger, Melvin) Putnam, 1985
Astronomy (Brown, Peter Lancaster) Facts On File, 1984
The New Atlas of the Universe (Moore, Patrick) Crown, 1984
Universe Guide to Stars and Planets (Ridpath, Ian) Universe, 1985
A Twenty-Fifth Anniversary Album of NASA (Vogt, Gregory) F. Watts, 1983

H.W. Wilson's Standard Catalog, latest edition

Societies
Joining an astronomical society will give you a chance to exchange views and learn about astronomy, and your library should have details of any local astronomical groups.

Places to visit
Planetariums
To get a really good view of the stars, you can go to a planetarium. There, moving pictures of the night sky are projected on the inside of a large dome. You can find out a lot about the universe at a planetarium, and a visit will help you to recognize constellations. Most large towns have a planetarium.
Adler Planetarium, Chicago, Illinois
National Air and Space Museum, Smithsonian, Washington, D.C.
Hansen Planetarium, Salt Lake City, Utah
Alabama Space and Rocket Center, Huntsville, Alabama
Fleischman Planetarium, Reno, Nevada
Klink Observatory, Lexington, Virginia
Franklin Institute Science Museum and Planetarium, Philadelphia, Pennsylvania

Observatories
Most observatories where professional astronomers work with telescopes are situated at the tops of high mountains and so are difficult to visit. However, some towns have small observatories at which you may be able to look through a big telescope at the heavens.

Radio telescopes
Radio telescopes do not need to be built on mountain tops and so can be visited easily.

◄ Arno Penzias (left) and Robert Wilson won the Nobel Prize for their discovery of radio waves in space. These may have been caused by the Big Bang.

280 B.C. Aristarchus first put forward the view that the Earth revolves around the Sun.
240 B.C. Eratosthenes first worked out the correct size of the Earth.
1054 Chinese astronomers recorded a supernova explosion in the constellation Taurus. The Crab Nebula is the remains of this event.
1543 Nicolaus Copernicus published his theory that the Earth and the other planets revolve around the Sun.
1608 Hans Lippershey invented the telescope.
1609 Johann Kepler discovered the laws that govern the orbits of the planets.

Important Discoveries

1785 William Herschel first attempted to describe our galaxy.

1801 Giuseppi Piazzi discovered the first asteroid, Ceres.

1846 Johann Galle discovered the planet Neptune.

1912 Vesto Slipher first observed the red shift.

1918 Harlow Shapley discovered the first galaxy outside our own galaxy.

1927 Georges Lemaitre first put forward the Big Bang theory.

1929 Edwin Hubble showed that the universe is expanding.

1610 Galileo began to make the first discoveries with the telescope. These included the four moons of Jupiter and the phases of Venus.

1668 Isaac Newton built the first known reflecting telescope.

1705 Edmond Halley successfully predicted the next appearance of Halley's comet, in 1758.

1728 James Bradley observed a slight movement of the stars caused by the Earth's motion around the Sun. This was the first scientific evidence that the Earth moves.

1781 William Herschel discovered the planet Uranus.

1930 Clyde Tombaugh discovered the planet Pluto.

1932 Karl Jansky discovered radio waves coming from space.

1957 The first satellite, Sputnik 1, went into orbit.

1959 The first space probe, Luna 3, photographed the Moon's hidden side.

1962 Mariner 2 flew past Venus.

1963 Maarten Schmidt identified the first quasar.

1965 The radiation in space predicted by the Big Bang theory was discovered by Arno Penzias and Robert Wilson.

– The space probe, Mariner 4, sent back the first close-up pictures of Mars.

1966 Luna 9 became the first probe to land on the Moon and send back pictures of the surface.

1967 Jocelyn Bell discovered the first pulsar.

1971 The first evidence of a black hole was discovered by an X-ray satellite.

1973 Pioneer 10 flew past Jupiter.

1974 Mariner 10 flew past Mercury.

1976 Viking 1 became the first space probe to land on Mars.

1979 Pioneer 11 flew past Saturn.

1983 The infra-red satellite IRAS began to map the heavens, leading to the discovery of solar systems around other stars.

Word List

Asteroid A small planet. Most asteroids orbit the Sun between Mars and Jupiter.

Astronomy The study of all the bodies in the universe, including the Sun, Moon, planets, stars and galaxies.

Big Bang The vast explosion that most astronomers think formed the universe about 15,000 million years ago.

Black Hole A body in space that swallows up everything around it, including light rays.

Body or heavenly body Any object in the universe, such as a moon, planet or star.

Comet A ball of gas and dust in the solar system. It forms a tail if it comes near the Sun.

Constellation A pattern of stars as seen in the night sky.

Double star A pair of stars that revolve around each other.

Eclipse A disappearance of a body caused by another body moving in front of it.

Energy The heat, light and radio waves given out by some stars and galaxies are forms of energy.

Galaxy A group of millions of stars. The galaxy, also called the Milky Way, is the group in which the Earth is located.

Gravity A force that causes two bodies to be pulled together. Everything has gravity.

Light year A measure of distance in astronomy that is equal to 5.878 trillion miles.

Meteoroid A piece of rock or metal moving in space.

Meteorite A meteoroid that falls to the Earth.

Milky Way The band of stars that crosses the sky. The galaxy is also called the Milky Way.

Molecule Molecules are groups of atoms, which are tiny particles only visible in the most powerful microscopes. Everything is made up of molecules or separate atoms. This page is about half a million atoms thick.

Moon A body that orbits a planet. Our Moon takes 27.32 days to orbit the Earth.

Naked eye Observing with the naked eye means observing without using an aid such as a telescope or binoculars.

Nebula A cloud of gas and dust in space. The plural of nebula is nebulae.

Nuclear fusion A process that occurs in stars and releases immense heat and other forms of energy.

Observatory A place or building where astronomers make observations of the heavens.

Orbit The path that a body takes as it moves through space around another body.

Phases The changes in shape that a moon or planet appears to undergo in its orbit.

Planet A world that is in orbit around the Sun or a star.

Pulsar A body that produces flashes of light or pulses of other rays.

Quadrant An ancient instrument used to measure the position of a star in the sky.

Quasar A kind of object that astronomers think is extremely bright and very distant from us. A quasar may possibly be the core of a remote galaxy.

Radio telescope An instrument that detects radio waves coming from space.

Red shift A change in the color of a star caused by its movement.

Satellite An automatic spacecraft that orbits the Earth.

Solar prominence An enormous outburst of blazing gas that forms briefly above the surface of the Sun. A prominence may be as much as 50,000 miles long.

Solar System The group of planets and moons, asteroids and comets that orbit the Sun. The Sun itself is also part of the solar system.

Space probe An automatic spacecraft that flies to the Moon or planets.

Star A globe of glowing gas like the Sun.

Sun The Sun is a star. It is 93 million miles from Earth and is 864,000 miles across. Its surface temperature is 6000 °C.

Supernova An exploding star.

Telescope A refracting telescope uses lenses to form a magnified image of an object. A reflecting telescope uses one or more curved mirrors.

Index